Hawaii Travel Guide
Top 10 places to Visit in Hawaii

Table of Contents

Introduction

Aloha! So, you're finally ready to embark on your much-awaited trip to Hawaii! We're very excited for you and want you to have the best experience on this iconic, mesmerizing island. This is why we've prepared this comprehensive and easy-to-understand guidebook that will tell you everything about traveling to Hawaii and its many destinations.

This tropical island known around the world is located in the Pacific Ocean and boasts white sandy beaches, clear water, gorgeous valleys, and outstanding mountain ranges. The cluster of islands is around 2,000 miles away from the U.S. mainland. Hawaii comprises 8 individual islands: Hawai'i, O'ahu, Maui, Lana'i, Koho'olawe, Moloka'i, Ni'ihau, and Kaua'i. These "high" islands give the archipelago its unique and eclectic character. Among them, O'ahu, home to Hawaii's capital Honolulu, is the most popular and inviting place. The diverse and culturally rich state blends influences from Korean, Japanese, Thai, Chinese, Samoan, Tongan, Portuguese, Spanish, Micronesian, and Tahitian heritage, making it a genuine and welcoming melting pot.

Historically, Hawaii was first inhabited by Polynesians who reached the islands in 400 C.E., using the night stars to navigate their way. As more and more explorers, navigators, and missionaries from Europe and East Asia converged towards the island territory, Hawaii witnessed many ups and downs until it was officially declared the 51st state of the United States of America in 1959.

Natives are proud of their heritage and culture, which is apparent in their way of living. The city names, the local language, and hula demonstrate how intact Hawaii culture has remained over the years. The cultural significance also gave birth to the state's delicious food scene. Hawaii's cuisine has emerged through the decades and includes remnants of every culture and nationality, guaranteeing you an unparalleled food experience. You should also try authentic Hawaiian cuisine, which is slowly gaining in popularity among visitors.

Hawaii revels in its untouched beauty. Many places have remained unchanged for centuries, whereas others have still been left undiscovered. If you want to relax and unwind in a secluded spot on any of the islands, simply drive around, and you are bound to find a scenic, isolated beauty spot (make sure you leave the spot clean when you depart to conform to the law and retain the region's "untouched" disposition.) If you have many days to spare and want to experience Hawaii inside out, you can indulge in various interesting activities such as shopping at the famous flea markets, watching the spectacular wildlife, or exploring the mountains and valleys. If you are up for an adventure, put on your hiking shoes and explore one of the picturesque trails nearby!

The locals in Hawaii are some of the happiest and friendliest people you will ever encounter. They will not only provide valuable suggestions but may also invite you for a drink. A sweet smile from a local can truly make your day. Tourists are always welcome, which is why vacationers dread leaving this place when it's time to return home.

So, whether you are traveling to Hawaii for relaxation or simply exploring a new destination, this tropical paradise will not disappoint you. It caters to all needs and has something for everyone. If you are traveling with your partner, this beautiful state will offer the best and most romantic experience of your life. This is also why many couples love visiting Hawaii for its private beaches, upscale resorts, and fancy restaurants.

The friendliness and warm vibe of this island state match its "Aloha spirit." Upon reaching Hawaii, you will feel the pleasant atmosphere tingling your senses, which will make your tropical retreat even brighter and more thrilling.

If you are excited, let's start this journey and plan your vacation to the most iconic American state!

Chapter 1: Top 10 Sites to Visit

With countless places to visit in Hawaii, narrowing down your search can be a daunting task, especially when you are short on time. In this chapter, we will cover the top 10 not to be missed vacation spots in Hawaii. Since they are located on different islands, you will also get a taste and character of the major islands in Hawaii.

Honolulu, Oahu

Start by exploring the capital of this state, Honolulu, located on Oahu Island. Do not forget to visit the Waikiki Neighborhood and Beach, two popular sites for tourists in Honolulu. The largest city in Hawaii offers a bustling urban vibe while being laid back at the same time. You can either relax on one of the beaches of Honolulu or spend your evening shopping in Waikiki. Duke Kahanamoku Beach is one of the most famous landings in the city and is great for surfers and tourists.

The name of one of Honolulu's famous suburbs, Waikiki, refers to "spouting waters" due to the old rivers that joined the oceans there in the past. This oceanfront stretch is filled with restaurants, shopping centers, resorts, and entertainment spots. In your free time, stroll around the Waikiki Beach Walk or visit the Waikiki Historic Trail to see the legendary surfboards as urban markers.

USS Arizona Memorial at Pearl Harbor, Oahu

Located in Honolulu, the USS Arizona Memorial is a reminder of WWII valor, along with other historic sites. The site attracts millions of locals and international visitors every year. Pearl Harbor is home to five of the nine historic sites related to the 1941 attack, along with the USS Oklahoma Memorial, the USS Utah Memorial, areas of Ford Island, Battleship Row, and the USS Arizona Memorial.

Remnants of the USS Arizona Memorial can be seen on a sunken ship as soon as you reach the site. Now, although the tour is free, you must reserve your spot in advance on-site, where it's usually crowded. Visit the Pearl Harbor Visitor Center and the Pacific Aviation Museum with its historic aircraft and aviation artifacts. For a thrilling experience, you can also access a flight simulator to land a plane on a carrier at the Center.

Na Pali Coast State Wilderness Park, Kauai

Located on the island of Kaua'i, the Na Pali Coast State boasts an incredible landscape and mountain range. The cliffs fold into each other to create a ripple effect. The beauty of this landscape has been portrayed in the classic movie Jurassic Park. Multiple waterfalls plummet down Mount Waialeale, the island's second-highest point. The waterfalls appear to be weeping, hence its name, the "Wall of Tears."

If you have the luxury, book yourself a helicopter ride to admire the scenic setting from the top. You can also book a boat ride or explore it on foot. If you are up for an adventure, hike up the Kalalau Trail to reach the valley's central point and carve your own path. In the past, the Hawaiian Ali'i (the regional royal clan) resided within these valleys and established their base at this site.

North Shore of Oahu, Oahu

Among all islands, Oahu is one of the best spots in Hawaii, according to seasoned travelers. The island's northern shore lies between Ka'ena Point and Kahuku Point, which are the eastern and western regions of Oahu, respectively. If you want to experience the best beach life of Hawaii, you must visit the North Shore of Oahu. The scenic coastlines and large waves attract beachgoers and surfers from all around the globe. Banzai Pipeline at Ehukai Beach and Waimea Bay are two popular surf spots at the North Shore of Oahu.

You can access the main point of the North Shore through Haleiwa, a historic town in Oahu. Once you have finished relaxing on the beach or trying your hand at surfing, you can indulge in the local food scene or go shopping in Haleiwa. The town is also famous for its shaved ice and garlic shrimp, which are available at local food stalls.

Haleakala National Park, Maui

The next island on your list is Maui, home to some of the most popular sites in all of Hawaii. Haleakala National Park is surrounded by the 10,023-ft tall Mt. Haleakala, which adds a significant character to the location. You can engage in several camping and hiking activities in the vicinity or simply stay until dusk to watch the breathtaking sunset. To make your trip easier, rent a car and drive all the way to the summit from Central Maui within 90 minutes.

If you are specifically visiting Haleakala National Park to watch the sunrise or sunset, be sure to load up on food, water, gas, and warm clothes. Book a local guided tour to learn more about Haleakala's topography, rich cultural stories, and history. Hosmer Grove & Supply Trails, Sliding Sands, Kaupo Gap, and Halemauu are some famous trails near this site.

Molokai's Kalaupapa National Historical Park, Maui

The Kalaupapa National Historical Park is named after Kalawao and Kalaupapa settlements that spread across the island. In the past, many residents suffered from Hansen's disease (or leprosy), which resulted in thousands of deaths. Since water and road access is prohibited at this attraction, you can take a mule ride or arrive on foot. The spectacular view down the cliff will make the ride worth your time and effort in reaching this remote site. Your mule will take you down one of the highest sea cliffs in the world until you reach Molokai Island.

Hawaii Volcanoes National Park, Big Island

Located on the southern end of Hilo, Hawaii Volcanoes National Park is known for its two famous volcanoes. The chance to see and learn about the creation and destruction process in one spot makes the National Park one of the most coveted attractions among tourists. Maunaloa and Kilauea are the two active volcanoes that erupted in 1984 and 2018, respectively.

Trip to Lanai, Maui

One of the lesser-visited islands of the lot, Lanai, is known for its raw beauty and pristine landscape. The rugged beaches and blue ocean add to Lanai's untouched beauty. You can easily spend an entire day or two in Lanai. Take a guided tour to explore the unseen side of the island or book a cruise to watch the dolphins. You can also take a snorkeling cruise or enjoy a walk on the beautiful beaches of Lanai.

Hanauma Bay Nature Preserve, Oahu

Located on the southern shore of Oahu, Hanauma Bay Nature Preserve exemplifies Hawaii's natural beauty through its volcanic cinder cone, underwater sea life, and beautiful reefs. You can either stroll on the beach or discover the region's marine life with a guided tour. In the past, this bay was a popular fishing ground for the locals, but this activity was soon reduced due to the diminishing fish population. Several regulations were imposed to let the fish replenish and balance the ocean's ecosystem. The Bay also invites you to swim or take a dive under professional guidance.

Waimea Canyon State Park, Kauai

This attraction is dubbed the "The Grand Canyon of the Pacific" and offers spectacular panoramic views of Kauai island. From the deep valleys, you can see and feel Hawaii's dramatic, wild interior. You can also hike or trek on one of the mountain trails that lead up to Kokee State Park. Take a well-deserved break and enjoy a picnic lunch on the cliff overlooking the valley. Entry to this site is free and friendly for hikers of all levels.

For longer stays and expedition journeys, don't hesitate to go island hopping in Hawaii and visit the sites mentioned here. If you simply want a relaxing vacation, head to one of the lesser-known or "untouched" islands to experience true beach life and live like a local.

Chapter 2: Top 10 Experiences

Visiting the above top 10 attractions will cover a major part of your itinerary in Hawaii. However, certain experiences and activities will show you the island's raw and authentic side, which will bring you closer to Hawaii's true character. When in Hawaii, spare a few hours to engage in these 10 top experiences.

Attend the Merrie Monarch Festival at Big Island

Hawaii is proud of its cultural identity and rich history and is keen on spreading it across the globe. Locals hold several festivals and events to celebrate their heritage and familiarize people with the Aloha spirit. The Merrie Monarch Festival at Big Island is one of the biggest cultural events in Hawaii, spanning over a week. King David Kalakaua, who was lovingly called the "Merrie Monarch," was the inspiration behind this festival. He was revered for his contributions to spreading Hawaiian arts, dances, and music to foreigners. This event is celebrated in the town of Hilo, where people engage in traditional hula dance, craft fairs, cultural performances, exhibitions, art shows, and free music. You can book tickets online to watch the coveted competition "Miss Aloha Hula."

Go Surfing

Surfing and Hawaii are intricately linked and showcase a rich history. According to historical records, Polynesians surfed on the Pacific since the 4th century A.D. Even if you are not a surfing enthusiast or have never surfed before, you must try it once when in Hawaii. Every island is home to amazing surfing spots that will invite you to hop on a surfboard and go up against the larger-than-life waves. Laniakea Beach and Puaena Point in Oahu, Shipwreck Beach and Kiahuna Beach in Kauai, Launiupoko State Wayside Park, and Lahaina Breakwall in Maui, and Honolii Beach Park and Kahaluu Beach in Big Island are visit-worthy spots for surfing in Hawaii. Some places even give lessons and allow you to rent a surfboard at an affordable price.

Go Night Diving with Mantas on Big Island

Another coveted water activity in Hawaii is night scuba diving and snorkeling. This once-in-a-lifetime experience allows you to swim with manta rays in the Pacific. Even if you cannot swim, the professional guides will ensure that you have the best and safest diving experience. You can swim and somersault with the manta rays during peak season, an experience that many travelers have had on their bucket lists for years. Kohala Coast, South of Kona, and North of Kona are three spots where you can meet these gentle giants and enjoy the best night diving experience.

Lay on the Beaches of South Maui

It goes without saying that your Hawaii vacation is incomplete without visiting the beautiful beaches of this tropical state. Since Hawaii is mainly known for its beaches, you must visit some of the most renowned sandy spots and dip your toes in the crystal-clear seawater. Of all islands, Maui is highly regarded for its beautiful beaches. If you are a beach lover, spare an extra day on this gorgeous island and explore all the famous and lesser-known beaches. Some of them include Ho'okipa, Kanaha Beach, Spreckelsville Beach, Baldwin Beach, and Pā'ia Secret Beach.

Go Volcano Biking

Bike your way straight to the Earth's center on Maui Island, also famous for its volcano eruptions. The Haleakala Crater retains the remains of volcanic eruptions and offers bikers a superb view. This downhill biking experience is a no-stress ride that will acquaint you with Hawaii's cool and tropical breeze. Take a guided tour to learn more about Hawaii and the island's volcanic history. Hop on to another adventure after your bike ride. Some services also offer zipline tours where you can enjoy the ocean's top view and see Hawaii from another grand perspective.

Try Snorkeling in Molokini

Shaped like a half-moon, the Molokini Crater invites swimming and snorkeling enthusiasts on a daily basis. Whether you are a novice or a professional, this site lets every type of snorkeler enjoy its turquoise water and colorful marine life. The crater basin has three levels, all of which are meant for different experience levels of divers. The 35-ft plateau is ideal for beginners, whereas the sloping wall at a depth of 70-ft is suitable for intermediate snorkelers. If you have enough experience with snorkeling or diving, you can go deeper into the crater water with proper supervision. From yellow butterflyfish to manta rays, you are bound to witness some spectacular marine life.

Rent a Party Bike Bar Tour in Honolulu

Hop on a party bike that carries 15 passengers at once and peddle around the Kakaako area with your friends. This new bar hop is one of the best ways to experience Hawaii's chill vibe during the day and at night. You will make three stops, including the Hibiscus Club and Honolulu Beerworks, to freshen up with a cool beer. Since the seats are limited and are often reserved, be sure to book your spot beforehand. You should definitely give it a "shot" if you are visiting Hawaii with a big group of friends!

Address: 311 Keawe St, Honolulu, HI 96813, USA

Go Horseback Riding on Kauai Island

Kauai boasts great open pastures that offer supervised horseback riding experiences. You get to ride across a working ranch with a waterfall pool and volcanic peaks as the backdrop. You will be greeted by the sweet smiles of the local cowboys known as "paniolo" and who often sing and smile to spread the Aloha spirit.

Try Your Hand at a Golf Game on the Mauna Kea Golf Course

One of the oldest in Hawaii, the Mauna Kea Golf Course can be accessed by reaching the Kohala Coast. The course is made of black lava, a result of old volcanic eruptions. The field welcomes championships and competitions and is one of the most popular courses in the state. Another popular golf resort is Kapalua and attracts national-level players during competitions. Every January, the PGA Mercedes Championship takes place at this very resort, which has also increased its popularity among seasonal visitors.

Visit the Princeville Botanical Gardens

These gardens grow several of the lesser-known types of flowers and medicinal plants, some of which can only be cultivated in Hawaii's tropical climate. You can take a guided tour to learn more about the region's exotic species and rare flora. Several places around the island show working beehives as well as cacao production.

Address: 3840 Ahonui Place, Princeville, Hawaii

Many of these activities are on every travel enthusiast's list and a superb way to rekindle your bond with nature. If you have been dreaming of scuba diving or surfing during one of your trips, now is your chance. The clear, blue waters of the Pacific invite you to explore them closely.

Chapter 3: Preparing for Hawaii

Once you have an idea of local sites and experiences, you must start preparing for your trip. In this chapter, we will take go through a comprehensive checklist for everything you must carry, things you should know, and some ways to get around Hawaii. Thorough preparation will guarantee you a safe, stress-free time on the island.

Things to Carry

While some of the basic things like UV-protected sunglasses and an extra set of clothes are essentials when traveling in general, you must pack certain items that are necessary for Hawaii.

1. Reef-Safe Sunscreen

According to new regulations, you cannot carry sunscreen that is not reef-safe. Certain chemicals in sunscreens are toxic to coral reefs and can threaten marine life. When buying sunscreen for your trip, check the ingredients listed in the products and ensure that they are reef-safe. A quick Google search can help you pick an adequate sunscreen. You can also purchase one once in Hawaii, as they have banned the sale of toxic sunscreens.

2. Quick-Dry T-shirts

Due to high temperatures and humidity, you need your outfits to be sweat-absorbing and moisture-wicking, especially if you are hiking or trekking. Instead of packing cotton t-shirts, buy a few quick-dry t-shirts to absorb sweat and keep you fresh all day. If you are planning on snorkeling, diving, or taking up any other water activity, invest in a UV-protected swim shirt to avoid harsh sunburn.

3. Hiking Sandals and Water Shoes

When in Hawaii, pay attention to your footwear according to your activity or the place you are visiting. While flip flops are ideal for the beach, you need special hiking sandals to climb up a cliff due to rough terrain. They provide a better grip and protect your feet from loose gravel. To walk on rockier beaches, wear special water shoes. These are also useful for snorkeling and swimming.

4. Swimming Goggles

Do not forget your swimming goggles if you plan to spend most of your time in the water. Clear glasses are best for visibility. For a proper snorkeling experience, get snorkeling gear or pack a snorkeling mask to stay underwater for longer periods. If you have less luggage space, you can spend a few extra bucks and rent or buy the full gear once in Hawaii.

5. Waterproof Bag and Phone Case

No one don't wants their phone or bag to get damaged, whether they are hiking or relaxing by the shore. Carry a simple waterproof bag and phone case to keep your items covered and protected. If you want to go diving and capture images underwater, you can use your waterproof phone case to safely use your camera.

6. Carry Your Own Sustainable Bags

Due to the threat of plastic to marine life and oceans, Hawaii has banned the use of single-use plastic. Instead of getting paper bags, invest in a high-quality cloth or reusable bag that can help reduce litter and limit the use of plastic.

These are some of the main things you should carry around with you. Apart from these, depending on your activity and/or location, add other basic travel essentials like toiletries, a hat, a first-aid kit, etc.

Things You Should Know

Before you start packing and planning your trip, there are certain factors to consider as they can impact your stay. From learning about the weather to getting to know the local mindset, these tips can fully prepare you for your trip to Hawaii.

What to Wear

The weather in Hawaii is predominantly warm and humid. It is common for locals and tourists to wear shorts and linen shirts or dresses. Carry a hat and a pair of sunglasses to protect yourself from harsh sun rays during summer. You may experience a little rain during the winter season, between November and March. If you are traveling then, plan your stay on the island's leeward side to stay dry and avoid the rain.

Pick Your Island Based on Your Vacation Goals

Since Hawaii offers a variety of flavors, every traveler visits the island with different expectations. Some may need relaxing time by the beach, whereas others may want to explore the fascinating landscape or take a road trip. Depending on your goals, you can pick the island of your choice. On the one hand, Kauai, Oahu, and Maui are the best islands to experience the authentic Hawaiin vibe. You can also find several beach resorts on these islands to relax and unwind. On the other hand, Big Island, Maui, and Molokai are the best spots to hike, snorkel, and dive.

Planning Your Budget

Here is an overview of how much you will spend before and during your trip.

- Inter-island flight: $50 to $100
- Car rental: $35 to $70 per day
- Accommodations: $40 to $50 per night for a dorm room, $50 to $100 per night for an Airbnb private room, and $120 to $250 per night for a single room in an upscale hotel or beach resort
- Restaurant meal: $15 to $30, plus tip
- Luau show: $75 to $120
- 2-tank dive: $120 to $180, plus equipment cost and taxes
- Surfing lesson: $75
- Shopping: $100 to $250 (can be excluded to save for a budget-friendly trip)
- Poke bowl: $12 to $15
- Fresh coconut: $5 to $8 (because your trip is incomplete without having a fresh Hawaiian coconut!)

These are some common expenses for tourists in Hawaii. Depending on your needs and vacation goals, your budget may differ.

Local Etiquette

Upon arrival, every guest is adorned with a lei (traditional flower necklace) and welcomed with a sweet "Aloha" by the locals. Rest a closed lei on your shoulders, with half of it draped down the back and the other half at the front. If the lei is untied or open, let it hang evenly around your neck. When visiting a Hawaiian's home, be sure to leave your slippers or footwear at the door before entering. During your visit, bring a gift, or omiyage, for the host. Learn some Hawaiian words as locals will appreciate your effort. Some of them are:

- mahalo: thank you
- e komo mai: welcome
- a hui hou: until we meet again
- kokua: help
- ono: delicious
- e kala mai i a`u: please forgive me (generally used for "I am sorry")

Ocean Safety and Marine Life Regulations

Despite being inviting and warm, the Pacific can be a life-threatening environment if you fail to heed warnings. This is especially important if you cannot swim. Always look for a lifeguard on the beach before you get into the water. When locals and lifeguards say, "Never turn your back to the ocean," listen to them. If the weather reports and beach signs warn you about hazardous conditions, do not get into the water. Be careful of box jellyfish, as their stings can cause deep rashes and swelling. Most importantly, do not touch marine life. Any level of human interaction or interference can be destructive to aquatic animals, as well as to you. Since it is illegal to feed, touch, or approach marine life, always be respectful and maintain a safe distance.

Getting Around Hawaii

One of the most important aspects to consider before traveling to Hawaii is the transportation offered. Since Hawaii is spread across 8 islands that lie far away from each other, you must know the right way to get to an island of your choice.

By Air

For successful island-hopping, you need to take a flight from one island to another. Hawaiian Airlines, Mokulele Airlines, and Southwest Airlines are some of the top operating airlines for these short itineraries. Typically, Oahu acts as the main hub for international and inter-island flights. A flight from Honolulu International Airport (HNL) takes around 30 to 45 minutes to reach another island. The only way to explore an extremely remote area like the Forbidden Island of Niihau is by helicopter. However, they can be expensive and swallow a major part of your budget.

By Ferry

Although ferries are not a popular choice, several services still operate between Lanai and Maui. A one-way ride costs around $30 and takes 45 to 60 minutes. Due to the limited frequency of ferry rides, you must book your ride in advance. If you are a sea lover who wants to explore the Pacific first-hand, taking a ferry ride instead of a flight is highly recommended. For a more luxurious experience, you can also book a cruise to explore the four major islands with an overnight stay.

By Car

There are only two ways to move from one island to another, namely by ferry and by air. Once you get to an island, you can rent a car and embark on a road trip. If you do not have a license, you can access the Oahu bus system that covers a major part of the island. Just be sure to compare the bus routes and determine whether you can reach every region you wish to visit by bus. You can also book a guided tour or rent a taxi for a more laid-back experience.

When planning your trip to Hawaii, prepare a checklist of essential items and gear to facilitate your packing process. Buy a local map to mark the spots of your pre-planned itinerary. More importantly, always check the weather and pack suitable clothing.

Chapter 4: Food Scene in Hawaii

Hawaii's food scene is one of the most acclaimed worldwide. As mentioned earlier, the region's culinary approach is rich and contains traces of various cultures and influences. With so many dishes and delicacies to try, you will never go hungry. From Hawaiian comfort food to vegan dishes, there is something for everyone. Even the pickiest eaters will enjoy the food and come back home with full bellies!

Authentic Hawaiian Food

A plate of authentic Hawaiian food will comprise laulau, poi, poke, kalua pig, and mac salad. Typically, you get chicken or pork laulau in ti leaves with a big scoop of rice and Lomi salmon. Some even add pipikaula, a kind of dried beef, on top. The dish is also accompanied by kalua pig and poi and finished with coconut cream and taro pudding, kulolo. Haupia is another famous coconut cream pudding that can be enjoyed before or after the meal. Cooks suggest mixing and matching the dish components as you like.

Where to Eat: From fine dining establishments to local food vendors, you can get a delicious plate of authentic Hawaiian food on almost every island. Helena's Hawaiian Food is a James Beard Award-winning eatery that offers the best authentic Hawaiian food. It is located in Honolulu and has been serving the locals and tourists for over 70 years now. Ethel's Grill and Rainbow Drive-In are two other restaurants famous for their authentic Hawaiian food.

Poke

In the Hawaiian language, poke means "to cut or slice," which gave birth to their popular dish with sliced fish topped with veggies and sauces. Typically, poke comprises raw fish cut in big chunks and seasoned with spices. You can select a wide range of fresh fish and seafood to make your poke's base. If you are indecisive, try the traditional Hawaiian poke. It is made with roasted and crushed kukui nuts (called inamona), seaweed (limu kohu), and Hawaiian salt.

Where to Eat: While you get poke almost everywhere in Hawaii, you must try your first dish at the best poke place in Honolulu, Ono Seafood. Da Poke Shack's takeout is another great place to enjoy a wide array of poke dishes by the beach. If you haven't tried the dish before, ask the vendor to share their specialty to have a pleasant first experience.

Malasada

Native to Portugal, this donut-shaped dessert is now a popular treat in Hawaii. Once served during celebrations, malasadas are now sold as a street treat. Unlike typical donuts, malasadas do not have a hole in the center. A traditional malasada donut is a deep-fried spherical dough rolled in sugar. You can get these fluffy and buttery treats filled with creams and custards of your choice. From a simple malasada to a tropical fruit filling donut, grab as many sweet treats as you can during your visit.

Where to Eat: If you are on Big Island, try some malasadas from Tex Drive-In and Punalu'u Bake Shop. The latter is famous for its tropical fruit filling, whereas the bakers at Tex Drive recommend their traditional version of malasadas. Penny's Malasadas, Pipeline Bakeshop & Creamery, and Leonard's Bakery in Oahu also serve some of the best and freshest malasadas on the island.

Acai Bowl

Also native to Brazil, acai bowls are made with fresh frozen açaí palm berries as the base. They are topped with paiai (pounded taro), granola, and fresh fruits like strawberries and bananas. This refreshing dessert is then topped with sliced nuts (optional) and drizzled with honey.

Where to Eat: While acai bowls are popular everywhere, you must visit a few places to have the best experience. Diamond Head Health Cove Bar, 808 Urban Bowls, and H.I. Cravings Mobile in Oahu are the best spots to enjoy an acai bowl. Do not forget to ask for recommendations on the most popular or unique versions.

Shave Ice

What's better than a bowl of shave (not "shaved") ice on a hot day in Hawaii? Do not confuse shave ice with snow cones, as both differ in texture and weight. Shave ice has a powdery texture that instantly melts in your mouth. It can be topped with a wide array of ingredients like azuki beans, mochi, ice cream, condensed milk, fruit syrup, freshly cut fruit, and many more. Grab a bowl of shave ice with your favorite toppings and enjoy it on a hot day by the beach.

Where to Eat: Uncle Clay's House of Pure Aloha, Matsumoto Shave Ice, Waiola Shave Ice, and Aloha General Store offers an impressive range of flavors and toppings with their light fluffy shave ice.

Loco Moco

Known as Hawaii's comfort food staple, Loco Moco is a beef patty served with rice and gravy. Some versions also include a fried egg on top. The runny yolk blends all the flavors together to give you a lip-smacking experience. This dish was allegedly invented around the 1940s and derived from the Spanish word, Loco, meaning "crazy." Some outsiders prefer calling this dish a "deconstructed burger," which the locals absolutely despise. Other versions swap the beef patty for a Portuguese sausage. The gravy typically consists of teriyaki sauce, stew, and chili as the base flavor.

Where to Eat: If you are on Big Island, try a Loco Moco at Cafe 100. With over 30 versions of this dish, ask the owner to suggest one based on your preferences. Forty Niner and Fatboy's Hawaii are two other spots where you can try the region's best Loco Moco.

Garlic Shrimp

You cannot travel to Hawaii without trying the local shrimp. Even though shrimp is not naturally found in the local waters, the locals farm shrimp and sell them. Garlic shrimp is the simplest yet tastiest version of this popular seafood and is sold at food trucks and fancy restaurants alike. The smell of curled shrimp doused in fragrant garlic pods will attract you from a distance and lure you into trying it once. These sautéed shrimps are typically served with a pile of rice and a buttery sauce.

Where to Eat: Famous Kahuku Shrimp Truck, Big Wave Shrimp, and Giovanni's Shrimp Truck are three of the best eateries to try garlic shrimp. The White Trucks at Giovanni's are the most popular among them all due to their heritage and generous portions. They serve soft and crispy shrimp along with a delicious sauce. Their neighbor, Romy's, also serves some of the freshest shrimp on the island as they run their own shrimp farm nearby.

Manapua

Manapua is a Hawaiian dumpling filled with pork or other savory flavors. Today, you can also find manapuas with sweet fillings. While the most common version of a manapua is steamed, some also prefer them fried or bakes. The soft dumpling resembles char siu bao, a traditional Chinese steamed pork bun. Their influence can be traced back to Cantonese culture in the 19th century. The pork filling is red-hued and gives the manapuas a distinct look. If possible, get a plate of manapuas that are hot and directly off the stove, as they are fluffy and delicious when served warm.

Where to Eat: Sing Cheong Yuan Bakery, Honolulu Kitchen, and Aiea Manapua & Snacks sell the best manapuas in Hawaii. When at Sing Cheong Yuan Bakery, give their mochi a try as well. You can also get a pack of premade manapuas at Lawai Menehune Food Mart, located on Kauai Island.

Huli Huli Chicken

Ernest Morgado, a poultry farmer in Hawaii, has been a staple for the locals ever since he invented this iconic dish. Huli Huli chicken is a local grilled teriyaki chicken with marinated sweet soy sauce. In Hawaiian, Huli means "to turn." During cooking, the chicken is flipped multiple times so that the soy sauce will caramelize and keep the meat from burning. The chef ensures that the chicken gets a nice glaze and a crispy texture without overcooking it. The caramelized sauce is called "Huli" sauce and is significant to the dish. It also contains traces of pineapple and ginger to resemble teriyaki sauce.

Where to Eat: Try this dish at Da Mexican Huli, Maui Mike's Fire-Roasted Chicken, or Mike's Huli Chicken in Oahu. All these places offer their own version of huli chicken, which are all a must-try.

Fresh Tropical Fruit

Needless to say, you have to try local tropical fruits such as mango, coconut, lychee, avocado, pineapple, and papaya when in Hawaii. You can easily find fresh fruit on almost every island.

Where to Eat: Get the freshest fruits at a local farmer's market. Some stalls even sell cut fruits topped with honey and cream.

If you are a seafood lover, you will absolutely love Hawaii as it has some of the freshest seafood produce. From fish tacos to cold-smoked Aku, you will get lip-smacking seafood at almost every corner of Hawaii. Did you know that Hawaii is also popular for its coffee? Take home some locally harvested Macadamia nuts along with a few chocolate bars made from Hawaiian-grown cacao beans. With so much culinary variety and countless eateries and restaurants to visit, you should indulge in a food spree without worrying about the calories. You're on vacation, so enjoy to your heart's content!

Chapter 5: Where to Stay

Generally speaking, finding suitable accommodations in Hawaii is not an insurmountable challenge. With so many options to choose from, you should narrow down your options beforehand depending on your travel needs and budget. More importantly, be sure to book accommodations well in advance to save money and avoid last-minute hassles.

Luxurious Stays

Hawaii is well known for its beach resorts and luxurious hotels. If you want to spend a relaxing vacation, and if your finances allow it, consider these top-notch resort options in Hawaii:

Andaz Maui at Wailea Resort, Maui

Located on Mokapu Beach, this 15-acre resort lies close to the Wailea shopping center. The open-air lobby and tropical vibes invite you to feel Hawaii in its truest character. The Aloha spirit is alive at this resort due to its openness and impressive interior design. Despite being relatively new and modern, the resort has managed to capture the "Hawaiian feel," which has made it a popular choice among international tourists. In your free time, you can jump into a private plunge pool or visit the spa for a relaxing massage and opulent body treatment.

Address: 3550 Wailea Alanui Dr, Wailea, HI 96753, United States

Price per Night: $1200 to $1700 (depending on seasonality and availability)

Alohilani Resort Waikiki Beach, Oahu

Formerly known as the Pacific Beach Hotel, this resort underwent a massive $125 million renovation and a face lift. It was inaugurated under the name "Alohilani" and redesigned to feel lighter and airier. As soon as you step into the quiet and serene lobby, you will forget the hubbub of Honolulu's bustling streets. It feels like entering another world where you can enjoy your free time in peace. The two-story oceanarium is the highlight of this hotel.

Address: 2490 Kalakaua Ave, Honolulu, HI 96815, United States

Price per Night: $300 to $600 (depending on the type of room)

Ko'a Kea Hotel & Resort at Poipu Beach, Kauai

Despite being dainty and smaller than other establishments, this resort at Kauai is still popular due to its serene and comfortable vibes. The resort just has 121 rooms that get booked fast during peak season, which is why you must be quick with the booking as well. If you are visiting Kauai Island, we recommend staying at this hotel, especially if you simply want to relax and enjoy a view of the ocean. Several swim-up bars and waterslides at the hotel are its main highlights.

Address: 2251 Poipu Rd, Koloa, HI 96756, United States

Price per Night: $600 to $900

Four Seasons Resort Lanai

Lanai City is not as huge as other typical Hawaiian Islands. However, the Four Seasons Resort is a considerable incentive to visit the authentic ocean side of the state and relax in peace. Surrounded by multiple streams, waterfalls, ponds, and gardens, this resort is speckled with gorgeous natural elements. In 2015, billionaire Larry Ellison converted a major part of Lanai city into this resort after purchasing the land and old property in 2012. From the internal gardens to the Polihua Beach, you can access almost every part of Lanai when staying at this resort.

Address: 1 Manele Bay Rd, Lanai City, HI 96763, United States

Price per Night: $1800 to $2800

Mauna Lani, Auberge Resorts Collection, Big Island

This resort on Big Island has been thriving for decades and is known for its exceptional amenities and service. From well-heeled families to artists, athletes, and celebrities, many VIPs take up residence at this resort when on Big Island. Despite a massive $200 million renovation, the resort has managed to retain its character and nostalgic vibe. In your free time, take a dip in the infinity pool or grab a bite at the Canoe House restaurant across the resort.

Address: 68-1400 Mauna Lani Dr, Waimea, HI 96743, United States

Price per Night: $1000 to $1500

Moana Surfrider, A Westin Resort & Spa, Oahu

Honolulu's first luxury hotel, Moana, was inaugurated in 1901 and is popularly known as the "First Lady of Waikiki." The property's history and distinct architecture earned it its enlistment on the National Register of Historic Places. The resort features design elements inspired by Bauhaus and Art Deco. A century-old Indian Banyan tree also stands in the courtyard and adds even more character and charm to the setting. You can either book a room in the modern section of the resort or explore the historic wing.

Address: 2365 Kalakaua Ave, Honolulu, HI 96815, United States

Price per Night: $400 to $1000

The Ritz-Carlton, Kapalua, Maui

Sitting near Kapalua Bay Beach, the Ritz-Carlton will provide the most relaxing Hawaiian experience you can dream of. Kapalua is a residential and resort community designed to accommodate a pair of luxury hotels, residences, restaurants, hiking trails, tennis courts, and golf courses. The topography blends naturally with Maui's character and invites you to experience its low-key Hawaiian vibe. In your free time, visit the Honolua Market near the resort to grab a bite or simply walk and take some pictures around the island.

Address: 1 Ritz Carlton Dr, Kapalua, HI 96761, United States

Price per Night: $1800 to $2000

Budget-Friendly

If you want to spend as little as possible on accommodations, Hawaii also offers several budget-friendly hotels and BnB options.

Hakuna Matata Hostel, Lahaina, Maui

For solo travelers who want to meet people while enjoying a comfortable stay, the Hakuna Matata Hostel on Maui is an ideal choice. You can choose between a single room or book a bed in a mixed dorm. You can meet people from all over the world, build friendships, and even explore the island together. The property is located in Lahaina and offers access to several activities, restaurants, shops, historic sites, and bus stops.

Address: 545A Front St, Maui, USA

Price per Night: $60 to $150

Hilo Hawaiian Hotel, Big Island

This eco-friendly retreat on Big Island offers shared and private rooms, both of which offer tropical vibes. The rooms are colorful and feature sweeping ocean views with Mauna Kea as the backdrop. Located two miles away from Hilo airport, this property allows access to some popular sites like the Hawaii Volcanoes National Park, Coconut Island, and Hilo Town.

Address: 71 Banyan Drive, Hilo, Island of Hawaii, HI 96720-4693

Price per Night: $225 approximately

Maui Seaside Hotel, Maui

Maui Seaside Hotel is an ideal choice for those who want upscale accommodations without splurging too much. The hotel features a pool, a lounge, and a bar for you to relax in during your free time. Adventurers can access the nearby Hookipa Beach to windsurf or visit the Iao State Park for hiking. If you want to explore Hawaii's rural side, ask the property manager for some local village tour recommendations. During your free time, catch up on a golf game at Maui Lani.

Address: 100 West Kaahumanu Avenue, Kahului, Maui, HI 96732-1607

Price per Night: $200 approximately

Kings' Land by Hilton Grand Vacations, Big Island

Located in the heart of Waikoloa, this hotel is nestled among lush, green Hawaiian plantations and golf courses. It allows access to the Kohala Coast and other popular sites on Big Island. The property offers suites with one and two bedrooms at affordable rates. The furnishings and amenities are designed in a tropical style to make the rooms more inviting. In your free time, relax by the pool or take a walk around the property to experience Waikola's cool breeze.

Address: 69-699 Waikoloa Beach Drive, Waikoloa, Island of Hawaii, HI 96738-5712

Price per Night: $250 to $300

Queen Kapiolani Hotel, Oahu

This property is located near Waikiki Beach and provides access to some main sites, including Waikiki Aquarium, Kapiolani Park, and Honolulu Zoo. The hotel is named after the state's last king's wife. In your spare time, visit the beach to surf or visit Diamond Crater Hike. Some rooms provide a view of the beach and the zoo. The property lets you rent a surfboard of your choice at an affordable rate.

Address: 150 Kapahulu Avenue Waikiki, Honolulu, Oahu, HI 96815-4097

Price per Night: $200 to $250

Plantation Hale Suites, Kauai

Set near Waipouli Beach and the Royal Coconut Coast, this property provides access to famous sites nearby that offer activity like surfing, horseback riding, golf, spa, tennis, and hiking. Opaekaa Falls, Wailua River, and Waimea Canyon are some popular sites that can be accessed from your suite. Whether you are traveling with your family or spending your honeymoon in Hawaii with your partner, this property offers the best amenities for every kind of traveler within an affordable range. The hotel also offers BBQ facilities and a pool.

Address: 525 Aleka Loop, Kapaa, Kauai, HI 96746-1496

Price per Night: $220 to $250

The beauty of the Hawaiian Islands is that they can cater to virtually every type of traveler, regardless of their budget. That said, if you want cheaper options and do not mind sharing your room with others, you can opt for a shared BnB that will cost no more than $50 per night.

Chapter 6: Things to Do for Leisure

From an alluring shopping scene to fascinating nightlife, Hawaii has it all. After visiting all the major attractions, you can use your leisure time to experience the state's raw side. Hawaii offers several cultural shows and complementary activities that will complete your trip.

Nightlife

While it's incredible during the day, Hawaii also gives out its tropical and cool vibe at night. As soon as the sun sets, all the islands in Hawaii take another form and completely immerse in a laid-back experience where locals and tourists sing, dance, drink, and share precious moments. People who prefer to spend a quiet evening simply walk along the shore or relax by the beach.

Movie Night, Sunset on the Beach

An integral part of the local nightlife, the movie "Sunset on the Beach" is aired on a 30-ft screen on Waikiki beach during the weekends. This tradition was started by Honolulu's former Mayor, Jeremy Harris, and is still perpetuated after 20 years. At times, local musicians perform to entertain the audience before the movie begins. You can also buy food from local vendors who set up their stalls near the venue. Currently, the frequency of this movie night has been reduced, so it's important to check the event date and get confirmation before planning your itinerary.

Hilton Hawaiian Village Friday Fireworks

If you are passing by the Hilton Hawaiian Village Resort, don't hesitate to attend their fireworks show every Friday. The colorful spectacle lasts for 20 minutes and illuminates the beach lagoon, projecting a beautiful reflection on the water. While waiting for the show to begin, you can watch the sunset on Duke Kahanamoku Beach, which is close to the resort. The beach also invites you to stroll along the coastline.

Hilo Town Tavern, Big Island

If you are on Big Island, don't miss Hilo Town Tavern, a popular club, and bar that offers the best live acts in the region. From comedy shows to magic performances, the venue surprises the guests every night. The tavern also features DJs and live music acts, which keep the visitors entertained. Keep an eye out for their happy hours to get the club's best drinks at a low price. If you just want to hang out with friends or travel companions, gather around the pool table for a few games or hop on the dance floor to enjoy the music beats.

Address: 168 Keawe St, Hilo, HI 96720, USA

Shopping

Whether you are looking for a sundress, local artisanal objects, or some souvenirs to take back home, Hawaii is a shopaholic's ultimate haven. Check out some of these recommendations.

International Market Place

Located in Waikiki, this shopping center has been in operation since the 1950s and attracts hundreds of visitors every day. From international luxury brands like Christian Louboutin, Rolex, and Burberry to local beachwear labels, you can find almost everything you need at the International Market Place. Don't hesitate to take a break and grab a quick bite at one of the restaurants inside the shopping center. The tropical gardens add to the market's rich character and keep the Aloha spirit alive.

Address: 2330 Kalakaua Ave, Honolulu, HI 96815, USA

Ala Moana Center

Hawaii's largest shopping mall, Ala Moana Center's open-air space, is ideal for a pleasant shopping experience. The 4-story complex is also the world's largest outdoor mall and is designed to allow customers to enjoy the island's tropical climate. With two large food courts and over 300 outlets, this is the place to visit should you need anything during your trip. The center is also home to several restaurants and department stores. You can also stay back to watch a free hula show, which takes place every day to attract tourists.

Address: 1450 Ala Moana Boulevard, Honolulu, HI 96814, USA

Waikiki Beach Walk

This spot is perfect for an evening stroll or to shop for your favorite items. The open-air promenade is located on Lewers Street near Waikiki Beach and allows tourists to walk freely while soaking in the cool evening air. You can also have a good time in one of the bars or restaurants along the promenade. This oceanfront shopping strip is a popular hangout place for the locals as well. If you want to visit the beach but don't have the gear for water activities, you can shop at stores like Sunshine Swimwear and Quiksilver. For music lovers, splurge on a ukulele at one of the stores or at least get a lesson from the store owner.

Address: 227 Lewers Street, Honolulu, HI 96815, USA

Beaches

Schedule at least 2 to 3 days to visit some of the best beaches in Hawaii, to go for a swim, and relax by the ocean. While we covered a few top attractions in the opening chapter, these three beaches deserve a place on your list.

Makena Beach, Maui

Commonly known as the "Big Beach" of Maui, Makena is an unmissable attraction on the island. Surrounded by tall trees, this beach is a secluded place where you can claim your own spot and unwind on the sandy cluster mixed with black lava. Makena Beach is as beautiful as Lahaina and Kaanapali but is less crowded, which gives you a chance to admire its beauty at ease. The beach is as long as a football field and stretches up to a mile. You can easily spend an entire day there.

Waimanalo Beach, Oahu

This paradisiac oceanfront is located far from the noisy urban streets of Waikiki and looks absolutely spotless. Dr. Stephen Leatherman (who is also famously known as "Dr. Beach") is an American geoscientist who has named Waimanalo Beach the best beach in the country, no less. The white sand and rich turquoise water are surrounded by tall ironwood trees, illustrating Hawaii's truest beauty. Spending a day or two by the beach feels like visiting paradise. With Waikiki as the starting point, drive for about 45 minutes to get to Waimanalo.

Tunnels Beach (Makua Beach), Kauai

This half-moon-shaped beach engulfs the water that touches the shore, forming tunnels. Huge green cliffs surround this beach and add to its character. The bone-white sand is perfect for walking on. If you are up for some water action, you can go for a swim or snorkel at this beach. Kitesurfing and windsurfing are some other popular activities that tourists partake in at Tunnels Beach. After that, have your lunch at the picnic table and wait until evening to watch the spectacular sunset.

Performing Arts and Events

Hawaii is home to various artists, musicians, dancers, and performers who proudly represent their heritage and promote Hawaiian culture. As a visitor, you mustn't miss some popular shows as people come to attend them from across the globe.

Kuhio Beach Hula Show

This free hula dance show is held at Kuhio Beach to attract tourists and keep the local culture alive. Depending on the weather and time of year, the show is held on weeknights and makes great entertainment with a music and dance show with space for hundreds of visitors. Hawaii selects the most talented halau hula performers for this show. They gather on the pa hula (hula mound) near the beach to perform. The beautiful dancers are adorned in their authentic outfits and lei to represent Polynesian culture.

Diamond Head Theatre

Formerly known as Honolulu Community Theatre, this community center opened in 1915 and has since been inviting performers of all calibers to help grow and entertain their audience. The theater offers dancing, singing, and acting classes to performing arts enthusiasts and has prospered as a distinct community for over a century. Keep an eye on their website for upcoming shows to book in advance.

Ka Moana Luau

Located on Oahu Island's Sea Life Park Hawaii, Ka Moana Luau hosts evening performances and proposes an extensive Polynesian menu. From authentic cuisine to traditional music and dance, the entertainers offer one the best cultural experiences to their audience which makes a memorable night. The viewers also get to participate in certain activities like lei making, ukulele playing, coconut-headband weaving, and hula lessons. The servers also encourage you to eat at your heart's content, which will satisfy anyone with a great appetite!

Fun Activities

Along with a great shopping scene and performing arts pride, Hawaii offers plenty of fun activities for visitors of all backgrounds.

Water Activities

Water activities like surfing, snorkeling, scuba diving, and swimming are popular on almost every Hawaiian island with dedicated lessons available to visitors. If you are a beginner who wants to enjoy a water activity, start by trying standup paddle boarding. Surfing and scuba diving are highly recommended in Hawaii. You can also take separate lessons on popular beaches. After that, book a boat ride and go whale watching. If you are up for some adrenaline, go parasailing.

Take a Tour of the Kauai Coffee Company

As mentioned, Hawaii is known for its coffee. Kauai Coffee Company, the country's largest coffee farm, lets you walk through their production unit and offers free tasting.

The tour guide will also explain the entire process of coffee production, from the plantation stage to the roasting of coffee beans. You can also try their special coffee flavors, including Hazelnut and Toasty Banana Nut Cream, Vanilla and Chocolate Macadamia Nut, and Coconut Caramel. After the tour, they also let you relax on their lanai and soak in the aromas of the coffee plantations. Take some authentic coffee home as a souvenir for your loved ones.

Ali'i Kula Lavender Museum

Situated in Maui, this farm cultivates over 45 varieties of lavender on Haleakala slopes. The working hours are from 10 AM to 4 PM, and you can access the farm for a small fee. To learn more about flower types and the site's history, you can take a paid walking tour. Sip on some warm lavender tea while strolling through the fragrant farm. You can purchase accessories and food items made with lavender, like lemongrass-lavender oil, lavender chocolate, lip balm, tea, and organic lavender shampoo and conditioner.

Conclusion

Congratulations on making it this far! Now that you've read about the main places and beaches to visit, things to do, foods to eat, and the places to stay in Hawaii, it is time to prepare your itinerary. With this information, let's prepare a plan to help you get started. If you're going on a 10-day trip to Hawaii, this is a sample of what your Hawaii itinerary could look like:

Day 1: Landing at Honolulu International Airport. Start your trip with Oahu until you get familiar with Hawaii's vibe and climate. Explore the Waikiki district, try some authentic Hawaiian food in Honolulu, and roam around the city at night.

Day 2: Head to the North Shore of Oahu to see the beaches. Depending on your accommodations, you may or may not have access to a private beach. If not, visit one of the beaches on the North Shore and go surfing or snorkeling.

Day 3: On the third day, you reach Kauai Island via an inter-island flight. Do try the recommended street food items in Oahu before leaving, though don't forget to try the malasadas at Leonard's! You will arrive in Kauai around noon. You can walk around the island, take pictures, explore its beaches, or go sightseeing. If you have the luxury, you can also book a helicopter ride for unparalleled views of the sunset.

Day 4: Visit the Napali Coast, Hanalei River, and popular beaches in Kauai. Go hiking on the Kalalau Trail. If you have enough time, you can also go sailing in Poipu.

Day 5: You will reach Maui Island via an inter-island flight. Upon arrival, you can either visit the Haleakala Volcano or go explore the beaches. Kamaole and Ka'anapali are two famous options. Go whale watching in Lahaina and spend your evening shopping and sampling Hawaiian cuisine.

Day 6: Take another day in Maui to visit the places you couldn't get to the previous day. If you haven't seen the impressive volcano yet, schedule this visit for this day. Go windsurfing on Ho'okipa Beach and go hiking on one of the Hana trails.

Day 7: After an early morning boat ride to Molokini, head towards the Big Island by taking an inter-island flight. Since you may not have enough time during the day, don't hesitate to explore the beaches, walk around the island, and grab some local food.

Day 8: You will explore the Kona side of the Big Island. Head to the Kealakekua Bay and book a boat ride or go snorkeling. If you're a group, you can also go kayaking. The area also offers some great trails for hiking.

Day 9: After the Kona side, time to explore the Hilo side of the Big Island. As you learned, Hilo is famous for its black sand beaches and volcanoes.

Day 10: On the last day, you can unwind or partake in an activity mentioned earlier. If you wish, you can add an extra day to your itinerary to enjoy a last day by the beach. Finally, head back to Oahu to get to Honolulu International Airport.

This sample itinerary sums up your entire trip. You can always customize your plan based on your travel needs, interests, and budget. Whether you are traveling with your family, partner, friends, or solo, this is a surefire plan that covers the major islands and popular spots. If possible, dedicate a few more days of your trip to seeing the unexplored side of Hawaii, especially if you are traveling solo. However, if you are short on days and budget, you can always come back! Hawaii's unrivaled charm and beauty will definitely compel you to return.

As with any destination, research and preparation will guarantee you a safe and pleasant stay. Plan your trip in a way that lets you enjoy the tropical state's beautiful beaches, alluring mountains, and breathtaking oceans. Do not forget to sample the delicious cuisine and indulge in their rich history. Travel enthusiasts recommend spending at least 10 days in Hawaii because there is simply so much to see and do. In fact, many travelers choose to extend their vacation by a week to cover their itinerary. Some even stay there for a few months at a time to soak in the Hawaiian sun and indulge in the Aloha spirit.

You are now fully prepared to embark on your exciting journey! Be sure to keep this book as a reference and recommended it to any friend or family member looking for a memorable tropical retreat. Good luck and safe travels!

How'd You Enjoy Reading Hawaii Travel Guide: Everything That You Ever Wanted to Know About Hawaii?

I want to say thank you for purchasing and reading this book! I hope

you enjoyed it and it's provided value to your life.

If you enjoyed reading this book and found some benefit in it, I'd

love your support and hope that you could take a moment to post

a review on Amazon. I'd love to hear from you, even if you have

feedback, as it'll help me in ensuring that I improve this book and

others in the future.

To leave your Amazon review, Please go to the My Book Page and Leave your Review there.

I want to let you know that your review is very important to me and

will help this book reach and impact more people's lives.

Thanks for your time and support!

References

A. (2020, September 24). 10 top-rated tourist attractions in Hawaii — acanela expeditions. Retrieved from Acanela.com website: https://www.acanela.com/blog/10-top-rated-tourist-attractions-in-hawaii

10 Best Beaches in Hawaii. (n.d.). Retrieved from Islands.com website: https://www.islands.com/10-best-beaches-in-hawaii/

10 things to know before your trip to Hawaii. (n.d.). Retrieved from Hawaiianairlines.com website: https://www.hawaiianairlines.com/trip-planning-guide/10-things-to-know-before-your-trip-to-hawaii

15 Top-Rated Tourist Attractions in Hawaii. (n.d.). Retrieved from Planetware.com website: https://www.planetware.com/tourist-attractions/hawaii-ushi.htm

20 hawai'i dishes you must try when traveling to the islands. (2016, September 9). Retrieved from Hawaiimagazine.com website: https://www.hawaiimagazine.com/20-hawaii-dishes-you-must-try-when-traveling-to-the-islands/

23 foods you must eat in Oahu, Hawaii. (2020, August 13). Retrieved from Thegoldenhouradventurer.com website: https://thegoldenhouradventurer.com/travel-tips/foodie-guides/must-eat-in-oahu/

Adventure vacation Hawaii packing list! What to pack for Hawaii + packing tips for carry-on ↓ Oahu - Maui - Big Island - Kauai. (2019, August 12). Retrieved from Flashpackingamerica.com website: https://www.flashpackingamerica.com/hawaii-travel/what-to-pack-for-hawaii-packing-list/

Best of Hawaii: 40 favorite sights and activities. (n.d.). Retrieved from Frommers.com website: https://www.frommers.com/slideshows/819965-best-of-hawaii-40-favorite-sights-and-activities

Carver, A. R. (2019). Waimea Canyon State Park: Blank-lined journal for Hawaii camping, hiking, fishing, hunting, kayaking, and all other outdoor activities. Independently Published.

Connell, S. K. (2012, April 24). Traditional Hawaiian food: Eat these 7 massively tasty dishes. Retrieved from Migrationology.com website: https://migrationology.com/traditional-hawaiian-food-dishes/

Derrick, V. C. (n.d.). Best places to surf in Hawaii. Retrieved from Hawaii-guide.com website: https://www.hawaii-guide.com/best-places-to-surf-in-hawaii

Everything you need to know about inter-island travel in Hawaii. (2019, December 26). Retrieved from Thepointsguy.com website: https://thepointsguy.com/guide/inter-island-travel-hawaii/

Manta ray snorkel and dive guide for Hawaii (Kailua Kona @ Big Island). (2011, April 6). Retrieved from Lovebigisland.com website: https://www.lovebigisland.com/big-island-manta-ray-night-dive/

Merrie Monarch Festival on the Big Island. (n.d.). Retrieved from Hawaii.com website: https://www.hawaii.com/big-island/events/merrie-monarch-festival-overview/

Morton, C. (2014, October 20). The best resorts in Hawaii: 2020 readers' choice awards. Retrieved from Condé Nast Traveler website: https://www.cntraveler.com/galleries/2014-10-20/top-25-resorts-in-hawaii

Oahu nightlife, Waikiki clubs, Honolulu Bars. (n.d.). Retrieved from Best-of-oahu.com website: https://www.best-of-oahu.com/oahu-nightlife.html

Our 23 FAVORITE beaches on Maui. (2021, February 8). Retrieved from Lovebigisland.com website: https://www.lovebigisland.com/maui/beaches/

The Culture Trip. (2017, June 23). 15 reasons why you should visit Hawaii at least once in your lifetime. Retrieved August 30, 2021, from Theculturetrip.com website: https://theculturetrip.com/north-america/usa/hawaii/articles/15-reasons-why-you-should-visit-hawaii-at-least-once-in-your-lifetime/

THE TOP 10 things to do in Hawaii. (n.d.). Retrieved from Viator.com website: https://www.viator.com/Hawaii/d278

Tomky, N. (n.d.). Going to Hawaii? 10 must-eat local specialties. Retrieved from Seriouseats.com website: https://www.seriouseats.com/hawaiian-cuisine-local-food-what-is-spam-musubi-poke-huli-huli-saimin

Top 10 places to Visit in Hawaii. (2014, September 10). Retrieved from Prideofmaui.com website: https://www.prideofmaui.com/blog/hawaii/top-10-places-visit-hawaii

Travels, A. (2021, June 26). Epic 10-day Hawaii itinerary. Retrieved from Arzotravels.com website: https://arzotravels.com/10-day-hawaii-itinerary/

Visit the Kauai coffee plantation. (2016, September 13). Retrieved from Kauaicoffee.com website: https://www.kauaicoffee.com/visit-the-kauai-coffee-estate/

Made in the USA
Las Vegas, NV
26 October 2021